Takara

ELEPHANT PRINCE
THE STORY OF GANESH

To a sweet god. Thank you.

—Amy Novesky

I lovingly dedicate this book to my eternal father His Divine Grace A.C. Bhaktivedanta Swami Prabhupada and to my dear husband Mark, who has been constant in my life. Thank you!

—Belgin K. Wedman

Mandala Publishing
3160 Kerner Blvd., Unit 108
San Rafael, CA 94901
Orders 800.688.2218
info@mandalapublishing.com
www.mandalapublishing.com

Designed by Insight Design
Printed in China through Palace Press International

10   9   8   7   6   5   4   3

Library of Congress Cataloging-in-Publication Data is available.

Artist's materials: watercolor, gouache and 23¾ karat gold leaf were used on Arches 140 lb. hot pressed watercolor paper for the full color paintings.

ISBN 978-1-88606916-9

ELEPHANT PRINCE
THE STORY OF GANESH

TEXT BY
AMY NOVESKY

ILLUSTRATIONS BY
BELGIN K. WEDMAN

MANDALA
PUBLISHING

"This is a story of India in a time of gods and goddesses," began a mother to her son, "and a boy who became the elephant prince. How did a boy come to have the head of an elephant? I will tell you."

In the heart of the continent was a small city of amber palaces and rose-colored temples, fragrant gardens and groves of sandalwood trees. The sun shone like gold and birds of every feather filled the air.

A girl named Parvati lived here with her family. She was a goddess and she was a princess, but she was also just a girl.

But Parvati was not like the other girls. She was always alone, daydreaming about the stories her mother and her mother's mother told her—stories of faraway places. She was more interested in stories than she was in boys.

Then she met Shiva. The great god's name made
her girlfriends cover their mouths with the ends of
their saris and tease her with their eyes. Parvati,
they giggled, must have been struck by an arrow
from the god of love.

Parvati thought Shiva was the loveliest of all. He was a brilliant shade of blue, and he wasn't like all the other boys. He had seen the world. In fact, he was responsible for giving shape to it a little bit at a time.

Shiva thought Parvati was beautiful and blessed. He liked that she was a princess but didn't act like one. It wasn't long before he asked her to marry him, and she said yes.

After the wedding, Parvati left her beloved home and went to live with Shiva atop a mountain high above the clouds. They were happy.

But because Shiva was busy building the world, he went away often, leaving Parvati all alone. Shiva always received a festive farewell. When he was gone, the silence in the palace was broken only by the cries of distant peacocks. Not even stories could fill the emptiness.

Parvati missed her home. She missed her family. What she wished for more than anything was to have a child. She wanted to be a mother.

Shiva wasn't ready yet to be a father, but he couldn't stand to see Parvati so sad. And so he told her that if she promised to think about her wish—and only this wish—for one year, it would come true.

Parvati happily promised, and then she traveled all the way to the Ganges. There she offered the sacred river a gift of one hundred glowing candles and thousands of flowers. Each day she dreamed of having a child.

One year later, just as Shiva had said, Parvati found a beautiful baby boy lying in her bed as if he'd always been there. His face was round and bright as a moon. Parvati lifted him high into the air. She loved him instantly.

"Is he the elephant prince?" asked the boy.

"Not just yet. There is more to this story," said his mother.

When the gods heard that a prince had been born,
they descended from the heavens to gather
around Parvati and her newborn son.

The Sun crossed the sky in a golden chariot driven
by the dawn. The Moon followed in a silver chariot,
pulling night behind. Then Mercury and Venus arrived.
Next came scarlet Mars and beautiful Jupiter. Last to
arrive was the blue planet Saturn—his name was Shani.

Parvati proudly showed her baby to each, and the gods smiled brightly upon him. Even Shiva beamed. But when Parvati came to Shani, the shy god lowered his head and turned away.

Parvati insisted he look. Shani couldn't bear to disappoint her. Slowly he turned and looked at the boy, and the boy smiled. Parvati smiled, too, but her joy soon turned to horror when she remembered that whatever powerful Shani gazes upon is destroyed. It was too late. Her child's head had turned to ash and blown away.

Parvati fell to the ground with her child in her arms and sobbed.

Then the god Vishnu stepped forward and
promised to bring the boy back to life.

On the back of an eagle, he flew to a jungle
where he found a wise, old elephant resting in a
bright clearing. When the elephant heard what
had happened, he bowed and offered his life to
save the boy.

Vishnu placed the elephant's great head carefully on the boy's shoulders. All the gods held their breath.

For a moment the world was silent and still except for the buzz of insects and the hush of birds' wings. Then to his mother's delight, the boy slowly opened his eyes and laughed. Sweet golden bees made a crown around his head.

The gods celebrated with a great feast.

Then, after they had eaten hundreds of sugar cakes and their bellies were full, they blessed the elephant prince. Each gave him a small gift: a garland of marigolds, a string of beads, a bowl of sweets, a parasol, a conch shell, a lotus. The Sun gave him a pair of ruby earrings, and the Moon, a pearl necklace. The Earth gave him a pet mouse.

And then the gods gave the boy a name: Ganesh, the elephant-headed one.

Parvati had a gift for him too: a silver pen and crystal bottles of colored inks.

Then, she told stories, stories her mother and her mother's mother had told her and stories of her very own, and Ganesh wrote them down.

"But what happened to the elephant?" the boy asked his mother.

"The elephant," she said, "will live forever."

"And the boy with the elephant's head?" he asked.

"Why," his mother smiled, "he is loved by all, but most of all by me."

This story seemed to please the elephant prince most, for he wrote it down word for word for word.

AUTHOR'S NOTE

Elephant Prince is a retelling of a well-known Hindu story of how the god Ganesh was born and how he came to have the head of an elephant. In the most familiar version, Parvati makes him from the earth and Shiva is so surprised to find a stranger in his home, he cut the boy's head off. The version in this story—Parvati wishing for a child and a remorseful god accidentally destroying the child's head—is inspired by an Indian text thousands of years old entitled, *Brahma Vaivarta Purana.*

Who is Ganesh? He is one of the most adored gods of Hinduism. He blesses and protects, and he grants wishes. He's never without his beloved bowl of sweets and his companion the rat. He is believed to be the scribe of the longest story of all time, the *Mahabharata.*

ILLUSTRATOR'S NOTE

The stylistic approach used to illustrate *Elephant Prince* was inspired by the Kangra school of painting developed in the Kangra Hills of Rajastan, India in the 16th century. Although gouache and watercolor medium was used instead of traditional ground pigments, the illustrator's focus was to try to capture the mood of Indian miniature paintings. It was a humbling and joyous experience. 23³⁄₄ karat gold leaf has been used for the embellishments throughout.